"Title To Please"

Bethany Humphries

BookLeaf Publishing
India | USA | UK

"Title To Go Here Please" © 2023 Bethany Humphries

All rights reserved.

No part of this publication may be reproduced, stored in a retrieval system, or transmitted, in any form or by any means, electronic, mechanical, photocopying, recording or otherwise, without the prior written permission of the presenters.

Bethany Humphries asserts the moral right to be identified as author of this work.

Presentation by *BookLeaf Publishing*

Web: www.bookleafpub.com

E-mail: info@bookleafpub.com

ISBN: 9789358314632

First edition 2023

My Last First Poem

I thought of a clever and ingenious plan
To make me stand out from the rest
So I decided when I began
To make sure my first poem was the best

In order to achieve this feat
I thought I'd leave this poem till last
Then I'd know the poems I had to beat
To make sure this poem did surpasse

Alas I now wish I knew
When I left this poem till today
That I'd have nothing left to do
No funny words left to say

So though you'll read this poem first
Please note the rest have better themes
This poem was the last I versed
And should probably stay that way it seems

Past/Future Me

To Past Me:
Thanks for never wanting to be in the photo
And thanks for never being too outspoken
Thanks for never trying to do something new
Like singing or dancing, or other things kids do
Thanks for always being a quiet voice of reason
Thanks for staying steady in every season
Thanks for always trying to just fit in
Too afraid to rock the boat and get bitten

I don't have to worry about an embarrassing memory
My history is coiled tightly like a noose around me
I don't have to worry what other people think of me
Because past me lived a life that was blissfully empty

To Future Me:
Take the photo
Be outspoken
Do whatever you want to do
Be someone completely new

Bogeyman

It's weird the things that stick with us
That stay with us like a red wine stain
That hide like shadows in the abyss
In the hippocampus of our brain

These memories that lie asleep unheard
Unthought and thought entirely forgotten
Until someone utters a random word
And suddenly it's there in the flesh "begotten"

And we have no recollection
Of why we feel a certain way
Just the whisper of an emotion
A feeling we can't explain

I used to have a fear from an old home
About a haunted shed
I was too scared to talk about it
And it left me with a sense of dread

Then one day whilst reminiscing
About that home we used to own
I uttered a sentence, a forgotten memory
Of something I'd forgotten I'd always known

"Of course I didn't go into the shed"
"Because of the bogeyman living there"
Silence followed, as one would expect
What a silly notion I'd thought to share

I'd been only young at that home
My brothers much older and wiser than me
Who'd convinced their sister of a bogeyman
And she'd believed them, being only three

It did not matter that I was older now
Much wiser than my brothers had been
I'd carried that dread and fear around
Because of the bogeyman inside of me

Last Minute

I'm a constant deadline dangler
hanging on till the eleventh hour
And when crunch time finally hits
I surge on through with untold power

When I reach the final boiling point
And I find myself in a jam
No matter how terrifying the Dunkirk
I'll have a contingency plan

I'll scrape on through till the morning
In a last ditch effort to get the job done
I'll keep going past the last sunset
Right back into the morning sun

Whether you call them goals or deadlines
Milestones, or a target date
I'll always be deadline dangler
Holding on till it's just too late

Interlude

I made a haiku
Because I didn't know what
To write for today

Journeying

You wouldn't open a book
And start one chapter from the ending
Missing all the gory narrative
The bad guy, already apprehended

You wouldn't start a meal
Two thirds way through the main
Missing the starters and aperitifs
It would all sound quite insane

You wouldn't watch a film
That's 15 minutes from the credits
Trying to deduce the plot
Working out all its good merits

Don't try to start life in the middle
With all the hard work already done
You'll miss all the plots and narratives
Just take time and have all the fun

Don't worry about the journey
About some self-imposed limit on time
Start the book at the preface
Read it thoroughly line by line

If I Saw You

If I saw you in the street, I'm not sure I'd recognise you
You'd probably have more wrinkles and more grey hair too
You'd probably have a different smile and a different point of view
You'd probably love me differently, not the way I still love you

If I saw you in the street, I'm not sure I'd even say hi
I'd probably turn the other way and hope you walk on by
I'd probably try to sail on through with my head held up high
I'd probably hope you don't see the tears I will not cry

If I saw you in the street, I'm not sure what I would do
You'd probably ask if I knew you
I'd probably say "I used to"

A poem from the heart

I thought I'd write a poem
Something from the heart
So I took mine out and placed it on the table
Ready for me to dissect
But the waiter asked me if I wouldn't mind putting it back
As it was upsetting the other customers

Flowers

Dad buys mum flowers when he goes to the local shop
They're usually the ones on offer that were nearly ready for the final chop
He's never needed a special reason, to bring them home to bloom
It's enough that mum loves them, that they brighten up her room

Worst Fear

I always thought my worst fear
Would be of something quite mundane
But I wonder if my worst fear
Is that I don't know when I should be afraid

I jump and quiver at every thought
At every decision I have to make
I fear every conversation I have had
And every one I have to make

I am afraid of things I've said
And things I'm not even sure I've done
I enjoy the party at the time
But then fear I've had too much fun

Should I be afraid of what I'm doing
Should I fear the time that is to come
Should I worry about the closing darkness
Should I stress over the blinding sun

My worst fear, I think it's fair to say
Is the life I lead every day

Explaining Poetry

Sometimes poems are long
With good use of literary devices
And sometimes they are short
And they don't even rhyme

My Demise

On the event of my demise
I need to make it perfectly clear
I am not in some grave or urn
I will not still be here

On the event of my demise
It should be well understood
I was happy with the life I led
All the bad and some of the good

On the event of my demise
However untimely it may seem
I'm happy with where I am
Where I will be and where I've been

On the event of my demise
Don't wallow in self-pity
The crying doesn't suit your eyes
And the snot won't make you pretty

On the event of my demise
Know my love will always be with you
Like a lighthouse in the storm
Guiding your way through

On the event of demise
Keep living though I'm out of sight
And when you're in the dark times
My love will guide you through the night

Anger

Anger has this annoying way
Of being exceptionally unhelpful

Your hands tremor
Your eyes water
Your brain burns

There is no focus
No logic
No thought

Just
Anger

The Road

The road I take is mine alone
Though others may come into roam
I cannot follow another's line
Just follow the path that is all mine

The road I take is long and short
Others take roads of another sort
I follow mine from start to end
Through every straight and every bend

The road I take is sometimes sad
But I'll meet people who make me glad
I'll meet some people who maybe bad
But mostly they will all be mad

The road I take has no shortcut
And the ending may be a bit abrupt
I have no choice but to follow through
It is the road I must pursue

The road I take is mine alone
But I'd be glad for you to come and roam
We follow along like parallel lines
Never crossing your path over mine

Strength

Sometimes there are words
Filling each expectant silence

Sometimes there are silences
Filled with the promise of words

And sometimes there are no words or silence
Just two hearts beating

He holds her hand
No words or silence

Just the knowledge
He is there

Blissfully Average

Some people are destined for greatness
To reach the highest mountain top

But I get altitude sickness
And cramps in my legs on long walks

So I'll stick with being mediocre
Sailing along on level ground

Someone needs to be average
To make the rest of you look so grand

Lightyear

It's quite a tranquil thing
To see the sky at night
To see the planets and the stars
Shining up there oh so bright

It's quite a tranquil thing
To see the stars aglow
To know you're looking at them
As they were so long ago

It's quite a tranquil thing
To be so close to the past
To know a light can shine forever
Keep traveling on so fast

It's quite a tranquil thing
To think that when I'm gone
You'll look into the night sky
And my light will travel on

Modern Day

When all these young folk
Talk in their modern way
I shake my head and wonder
Was I like that in my day?

Then I remember
No, I wasn't
I was too pedantic for all that

Time Well Spent Haiku

If I spent as much
time living life as I did
writing this poem

I'd have lived very
Little of my life indeed
Because this is short

Poetical Punctuation

If you've noted the lack of punctuation…
In the poems you've read till now!
It's less to do with the subject matter,
And more because I don't know how;

So I'll make up for it in this poem'
Give different punctuation to each line)
Don't be bothered by the oddity(
I'll still ensure I make it rhyme*

My Last Poem

My Last Poem Should Be My Magnum Opus
My Greatest Masterpiece
But I Put Too Much Stock In The Rest Of Them
Alas This One's A Little Off Beat

I'll Redeem It With Capital Letters
With My Ballad Stanza Rhyme
And Hope It Gives You A Little Amusement
So You've Not Waste Your Time

Milton Keynes UK
Ingram Content Group UK Ltd.
UKHW020918300424
441987UK00015B/744

9 789358 314632

Somewhere over the rainbow

Adele Mann

Somewhere over the rainbow © 2023 Adele Mann

All rights reserved.

No part of this publication may be reproduced, stored in a retrieval system, or transmitted, in any form or by any means, electronic, mechanical, photocopying, recording or otherwise, without the prior written permission of the presenters.

Adele Mann asserts the moral right to be identified as author of this work.

Presentation by *BookLeaf Publishing*

Web: www.bookleafpub.com

E-mail: info@bookleafpub.com

ISBN: 9789358319712

First edition 2023

To my Husband...for being my best friend, my rock and my soul mate

To Sophie...You are our sunshine on the darkest days and the most amazing little girl.

To Lottie...we love you so much and wish you were here with us but hope you're having fun dancing amongst the stars

And to our growing little bean - we love you already!

Our Lottie Rose

Our little Lottie, so precious and sweet
Wanted so badly but it wasn't to be.
Too good for this Earth, you were needed elsewhere
But that doesnt ease the pain and despair.
Our dear Lottie Rose, come sunshine and rain
You'll be loved and remembered until we meet again.

It still beats on

The sun shines on
A new day dawns
You awake in the morning
With a stretch and a yawn
Your heart still aches
For a piece of its missing
A piece so precious
But wait, just listen
It still beats on
It has life to live
Moments to cherish
And love to give
So feel the pain
Shout, scream or cry
But don't stand and watch
This life pass you by.

Butterflies

Freedom and beauty.
They flutter all around us.
White, purple and red.

Signs

A Robin, a feather,
a butterfly too
They all come to visit
And I know it's you.
The song on the radio
Playing loud and clear
Just you reminding me
That you are near.
The warmth of the sun
A whisper in the breeze
You're all around us
Amongst the flowers and trees.

The Candle

Flame flickers brightly.
Shadows dance all around us.
The room all a-glow.

That fateful day

A bright August day.
Full of promise and laughter.
How a day can change.

Rainbow

A rainbow so bright
It lights up the sky
With colours a plenty
So clear to the eye.
There's red and there's orange
There's yellow and green
Blue, indigo and violet
They all can be seen.
A rainbow of hope
An arch of dreams
Visions and wishes
That only you have seen.
A smile appears
As the rainbow joy spreads
Replacing the feelings
Of sorrow and dread.
A rainbow is made with the sun and the rain
Reminding us all that there can be joy amongst pain
We may be sad now, we my cry endless tears
But there'll be times of happiness in the coming years.

The peace in nature

Sitting by the lake
Reflections dance around
Of butterflies and dragonflies
As the fish swim up and down.
The gentle movement of the water
Brings a sense of calm and peace
It's nice to feel tranquility
Even for a short time, at least.
A ripple in the water
From a pebble dropped from high
The culprit then flies over
Making circles in the sky.
Flying freely through the wind
The serenity this brings
Watching as you fly away
With the wind beneath your wings.

Sophie

A ray of hope, our beacon of light
Making the darkest of days shine bright.
Her joyous smile and infectious giggles
Her raving dance moves and little wiggles.
The sound of her voice as she chatters away
Telling stories about her day.
The "I love yous" and kisses, the hugs and the cuddles
The joy when she gets to jump in the puddles.
Her love of helping out, cleaning and sweeping
And rocking her teddies when they are sleeping.
Reading, swimming and scooting along
Her sweet little voice as she sings a sweet song.
You made me a mum, my first born girl
You are our everything, you are our world!

Little Robin Redbreast

Little Robin redbreast
What have you come to say?
No, will you please stay a while
Please don't fly away.
Tell me all your stories
Tales of where you have been
Tell me of the all the beautiful things
Your tiny dark eyes have seen.
Just sit by me for a while
Your presence is needed greatly
It brings a warmth into my heart
There's someone I've been missing lately.
I know you need to fly now
Please visit me again soon
Until then I'll search for the one I miss
Amongst the stars and moon.

Firsts

The first breath you take
Waking on the first morning
Your heart is breaking
But a new day is dawning.
The first ride in a car
The first meal you eat
So hard to swallow
As your heart struggles to beat.
The first conversation
Full of heartache and pain
Wondering if you'll ever
Be able to speak again.
The first christmas, the first birthday
All the other anniversaries too
Leave you feeling the pain all over again
And wondering why this happened to you.
All the firsts hurt, there is no denying
But you will get through them and keep on surviving!

I wish

I wish I'd got to see
The colour of your eyes
Would they have been brown like the earth
Or blue like the skies?
I wish I'd got to feel your breath
The warmth upon my cheek
To hear you murmur and gurgle
Babble, laugh and speak
I wish I'd got to see you crawl
Stand and walk and run
And see you playing with your toys
Having lots of fun
Instead your up there in the heavens
Playing amongst the stars
I hope you know sweet darling girl
How very loved you are.

Grief

Like the waves of an ocean
It ebbs and it flows
It grows and subsides again
But never really goes.
It creeps up behind us
When it's expected least
Like an unsuspecting monster
An unwanted beast.
Your lives grow up around it
You learn it's OK to feel
But it never disappears
Time does not heal.

Feathers

Floating to the ground.
So complex yet so simple.
Feel your spirit near.

Love is...

Intense joy
The hardest pain
Laughing in the sunshine
Crying in the rain
Coming together, not drifting apart
The fullness, yet emptiness of your heart.

From behind the clouds

From behind the clouds
The sun rays shine
Radiating brightness
In the darkening skies
The power of the sun
Always finds a way
A small moment of warmth
On a dreary day
Just like our feelings
It's OK to smile
But don't be surprised if
This takes a while
But then don't feel the guilt
When these moments appear
Let the smiles happen
There's always time for tears
Our joy is just a lifejacket
Keeping us afloat
Amongst the ocean of cries
On board the grief boat.

Our Star

Which star are you?
Shining so bright
Lighting the sky
On this November night
So many stars
Twinkling away
I look up and wonder
And this is what I say
"Hello my sweet girl
I know you are there
Twinkling so brightly
Without a care
Keep shining my girl
For the world to see
For you'll always be
The brightest star to me!"

Our unborn child

As I sit here and write
My minds in a spin
The feelings...So many
I don't know where to begin
I'm elated, so happy
But so anxious too
Not knowing whether
We'll get to keep you
A size of a sweet pea
So incredibly tiny
But I can almost feel
Your energy inside me
I hope you'll grow strong
And come June or July
We'll have you in our arms
Soothing your cries
You're so very wanted
You're so very loved
Our little rainbow
Our gift from above.

My Lottie

"written with the words of Sophie"

I miss my Lottie
I want her here
I want to play with her
I want to show her how to do things
I want to feed her breakfast
I want to give her milk
I want to cuddle her
Why has she gone?
I miss my Lottie

Life

Live for every moment, as
If it was your last
For it is so fragile
Embrace, enjoy and laugh!

An ode to my husband

My best friend, my soulmate
My partner in life
My husband, my rock
I love being his wife.
Our hearts entwined
We were meant to be
From that very first moment
When we met for coffee
Stronger than steel
Our bond is unbreakable
The love we have for each other
Is completely unshakeable.
What we have is special
The love that we share
It's precious and priceless
It's incredibly rare
Love you more than all the world
You're my man and I'm your girl!

Milton Keynes UK
Ingram Content Group UK Ltd.
UKHW020918300424
441987UK00015B/745